TONBRIDGE

A Pictorial History

The Coat of Arms of Tonbridge and Malling Borough

Shield: The red crossbar and the blue vertical line represent a heraldic T and depict the river Medway flowing under the great bridge at Tonbridge and downstream into the Malling area, which is represented by a black heraldic M.

(*Official heraldic description:* Argent—a chief embattled of three gules between the centre of which a pale wavy azure. In base two inverted piles sable).

Crest: The Invicta or Kentish horse shows that the borough is in Kent, with the horse's neck entwined with a wreath of hops. The horse is mounted on a tower which is symbolic of the ancient abbeys and castles which make an important historic contribution to the amenities of the borough (e.g. Tonbridge Castle, Malling Abbey, Leybourne Castle, Aylesford Friary).

Mantling: Argent and gules (silver and red).

Motto: "Forward in unison" which expresses the desire of this Council for the Borough to go forward as an entity and to plan for the future needs of the Borough as a whole.

TONBRIDGE
A Pictorial History

Ivan Green

Phillimore

1990

Published by
PHILLIMORE & CO. LTD.
Shopwyke Hall, Chichester, Sussex

ISBN 0 85033 734 8

Printed and bound, in Great Britain by
BIDDLES LTD.
Guildford, Surrey

To Margaret

List of Illustrations

Illustration Acknowledgements

In addition to the collection of old pictures and drawings which I have accumulated over many years, and photographs I have more recently taken and processed, I acknowledge with grateful thanks the sources of others: the borough of Tonbridge and Malling, *frontispiece*, 32, 41, 58-65, 67-70, 72, 80, 94, 140, 150-3, 164-7, 174-5; the Community Services Department of the Kent County Constabulary, 26-9; Tonbridge School, 76, 106-7, 109-114, 117; Kent Fire Service, 25; the parish church of St Peter and St Paul, 83-5, 104; the parish church of St Stephen, 87-8, 92; the Tonbridge branch of the Kent Library Service, 98, 100; Whitefriars Press, 132-5; the Tonbridge headquarters of the National Rivers Authority, 145; Geoffrey Taylor, 119, 121-3; Brian Barnes, 164; Daphne Hoggett, 165; George E. Hall, 137-9.

Acknowledgements

I should like to record my grateful thanks to the many people and organisations who have helped in so many ways during the production of this book. I should especially like to thank the mayor, Councillor Mrs. Billie Sinlair-Lee, whose year of office coincided with the final stages of production; Councillor Barry Hughes, the borough's first mayor; and the deputy chief executive of Tonbridge and Malling borough, Peter Hopgood, through whose good offices the various departments of the borough organisation gave me enormous help.

I record my thanks for the official permission granted to reproduce my photographs of the borough coat of arms and the charter documents.

I am particularly grateful to Sheila Kostryka, the Information Centre manager, Julia Beilby, Ruth Whyte and Christine Palmer, all of whom welcomed my many queries and became personal friends. I was also guided and helped in many ways by John de Knop whose wise advice prevented me from making a number of mistakes.

Of the many others to whom I am grateful for help freely given, mention must be made of Mr. C. H. D. Everett, C.B.E., the headmaster of Tonbridge School, who generously opened the school and its library to me; of Geoffrey Taylor who allowed me to include illustrations he used in his new book *The Judd School 1888-1988*; and of Hilary Streeter and Wendy Wise of the Tonbridge branch of the Kent County Library.

Such busy people as David Underhill and Maurine Parker of the Whitefriars Press, G. Simmonds, Ted Rogans of the Tonbridge section of the National Rivers Authority, and Sgt. Peter Dunk of the Kent County Constabulary, all cheerfully gave their valuable time.

Brian Barnes, George Hall and Daphne Hoggett were generous in their provision of pictures and information, as were Mary Stevens, Stephen Carswell and Dr. Richard Stevens. The officers and voluntary workers of the parish churches of St Peter and St Paul and of St Stephen, including the verger, Doris Manser, all contributed in many ways.

There were many others, not mentioned here by name, all of whom I would like to thank for their help. Finally, mention must be made of those tolerant people who created this book from the writer's miscellaneous material, the staff of the publishers, Phillimore and Company.

Introduction

Tonbridge, a prosperous business, market and residential town, lies near the foot of sandstone hills of the central Weald, and in an area of Wealden clay. It straddles the Medway, Kent's most important river, at the upper limit of its useful navigation. At this point the Medway branched out into a number of shallow streams which formed the ford used by travellers from time immemorial when they trod the ancient trackway from London to Hastings and Rye.

Of the very early history of the town little is recorded, though the banks beside the sweet water river in the great Wealden forest must always have offered very desirable living places. To the south-east is Castle Hill, some 400 feet above sea level, where traces of mesolithic and neolithic man have been unearthed, along with the remains of two Iron Age forts, the holders of which would have been able to dominate the surrounding area, the old trackway and the ford in the valley, now the site of the modern town.

The life of the very early residents, living in their little thatched huts round the ford and on the banks of the small streams, is of course largely unknown to us. They would have employed very simple methods of agriculture, the gathering of fruits and edible plants from the great forest surrounding them, some hunting, and fishing in the many streams. There is no evidence of any pre-Conquest feudal system, and the community may well have been self-governing.

By the later years of the Saxon period much of the ancient forest had been cleared and the village had grown up round the old ford. No such village is listed in its own right in Domesday Book nor in the Domesday Monachorum, though there is a reference to it under Southfleet, in the record of the holdings of the Bishop of Rochester. This reads: 'In Tonbridge there is as much woodland and land from this manor as is assessed at 20s.' Too much should not be read into the absence of a record of a manor at Tonbridge, however, since others were similarly overlooked.

In the little village of Tonbridge was a small church, the remains of which are probably to be seen in the crude masonry of the north wall of the chancel of the parish church today. This early work is very probably the remains of the Saxon church of Tonebrigga, listed in the *Textus Roffensis*, identified as Tonbridge by Dr. Gordon Ward, who was a great authority on the Saxon and early Norman records of Kent.

Following the Battle of Hastings, William had to subdue and hold his newly conquered kingdom. His chief weapon was the castle. Construction was simple. Upon the chosen site an inner and an outer circle were drawn from a single centre. Local forced labour was rounded up and put to work digging the soil out from the space between the two circles and piling it up in the inner circle. As the space between the two circles became deeper, so the new artificial hill inside the inner circle became higher. The final result was a large conical hill surrounded by a deep ditch or moat which was dry if no water was available, and wet if there was a convenient water supply. At Tonbridge the water for a wet moat was provided by the river beside which it was built. The top of the artificial hill (or motte) was levelled off and the flat area created was encircled by a wooden palisade, inside which the lord's house and accommodation for his personal guard was erected. An outer palisade, enclosing the moat, and a bridge over it leading to a path up the side of the motte, completed the initial construction. Later, an outer palisade, enclosing a bigger area called a bailey, provided accommodation for the lord's hired mercenaries. Tonbridge's motte and bailey is the most complete example of this type of castle to survive in Kent, though remains of others can still be seen, notably at Folkestone, Stockbury and Thurnham.

The Tonbridge motte and bailey was built soon after the Conquest by Richard of Tonbridge, who was related to William and fought with him at Hastings. It served two principal purposes – to keep in subjection the people of the partly settled Wealden area and the people living in the local communities, and to safeguard the important river ford on the old trackway leading from London to Hastings and Rye.

Richard of Tonbridge was the son of Count Gilbert de Brionne and founder of the family of Clare, so named because of holdings in Clare in Suffolk. He was granted extensive lands in various parts of the country, particularly in Kent, and these are detailed in Domesday Book. He also held the Lowy of Tonbridge for the defence of Tonbridge Castle. The Lowy lands consisted of an area surrounding the castle, though it was not continuous because other holdings previously granted to others intruded into it in places.

In 1087 the Conqueror died, and in the following year his half-brother Odo (who had been banished by the king) returned to England and was joined by some of the English barons in his revolt against William Rufus. Tonbridge Castle was held for Odo by Richard de Tonbridge and his son, Gilbert de Clare, and it was attacked and captured by the king's forces after a siege of only two days. As a result, Richard was banished though his son Gilbert was pardoned. This was the first of a number of occasions when the holders of the castle featured in serious disaffection against the Crown. When the quarrels of their overlords led to open violence and war the people of the village, their families and homes were all in great danger.

In the late 11th century or first half of the 12th century the little church was rebuilt, and the present chancel was erected on the remains of the earlier Saxon work. Several of the old windows still survive to this day.

At around the same time the castle was destroyed by fire, but it is not known whether this was the result of the siege, a punitive measure afterwards, or an accident. This fire probably destroyed the old wooden buildings and the palisade at the top of the motte. Rebuilding was carried out in the improved style then coming into favour, in the form of a shell keep, the old wooden palisade on the top of the motte being replaced by a strong stone wall, parts of which still survive.

Also in the first half of the 12th century, the Priory of St Mary Magdalene for canons regular of the Order of St Augustine was founded by Richard de Clare, a descendant of the original Richard de Tonbridge. During the same period he also founded an identical priory at Clare in Suffolk. The site chosen for the Tonbridge priory was a little to the south of the ford and was, at that time, out in the country, well away from the little village round the ford and the castle nearby. It was not a very desirable area, being very low, intersected by streams and very frequently flooded in wet seasons. The exact date of its foundation is uncertain, different authorities suggesting different times, but early charters of c.1135 and c.1180 were followed by a papal bull of confirmation in 1191. The priory prospered, acquiring further lands during succeeding years.

In 1152 Roger, Earl of Hereford and Clare, held the castle and was soon at odds with that troublesome prelate, Archbishop Becket. Roger refused to pay homage to Becket for his castle, and the Archbishop sent an official messenger carrying the demand for compliance. There are several accounts of the encounter between the two men. One states that Roger received the Archbishop's messenger and compelled him to eat the summons, parchment and seal together!

Also in the middle of the same century, or perhaps somewhat later, the parish church was enlarged by the addition of a nave on the site of the present one, and a pointed chancel arch, probably the one which still exists today.

Roger's grandson, Gilbert, was present at the meeting of the barons at Bury St Edmunds to demand the preservation of their rights and privileges, a demand which led to King John being forced to sign the Magna Carta. The king's revenge was immediate and Gilbert was one of those to feel it. Falcacius, the captain of a band of mercenary soldiers, attacked and seized Tonbridge Castle at the king's command and held it. It was not to be released until after the king's death. Gilbert, however, regained royal favour and was with Henry III's army on the continent, where he died. His son and heir being only eight years old, the king appointed that great servant of England, Hubert de Burgh, Lord Warden of the Cinque Ports, Governor of Dover Castle and victor of many bitter conflicts with the French, to be Custodian of Tonbridge Castle during the period of minority.

The priory became increasingly prosperous and influential and in 1267 the prior and sub prior were asked by the prior and brethren of the Hospital of St John of Jerusalem, who held the advowson, to induct the new priest to the parish church of SS Peter and Paul, Tonbridge. In consequence, Brother Henry was inducted to its corporal possession 'by the delivery of a chalice and the key of the said church'.

In 1264 the castle, held for Simon de Montfort, was captured for the king, and the townsfolk suffered badly, as indeed they did so often during those troubled times. Their little town was burnt and, it seems, completely destroyed. The holders of the castle, the Clares, were well known for their unreliability and in August 1270, before Prince Edward sailed for the Crusades, he demanded the surrender of the castle as a surety for the continued loyalty and good behaviour of de Clare, Earl of Gloucester, while he was away overseas. Trust, however, seems to have been restored since, several years later, Tonbridge was honoured by a royal visit when King Edward I and his queen were entertained there on their way home from the Holy Land.

It was at this time that the castle was transformed into a considerably more efficient defensive fortification, the high stone bailey walls replacing earlier ones, the southern part of the new bailey wall lining the river bank, and the northern part being provided with a very strong entrance gateway which also formed a residence. The commander may have lived in this gatehouse, from which he could control the entrance to the interior bailey and also influence events in the surrounding countryside. This was in line with the new ideas of active, rather than passive, defence. This great gatehouse, built of blocks of sandstone, which was plentiful in the district, rose three storeys high inside a deep outer moat which was crossed by a drawbridge. On the ground floor the central through-passage was protected by great doors, guardrooms and portcullises, the machinery for working these being housed in the middle storey. Much of the top storey was taken up by the great hall, and the roof walk provided extensive views over the little town, the river and its ford, and the surrounding countryside.

Built into the eastern wall of the bailey were two towers, mentioned in a 16th-century document as the water tower at its southern end and the Stafford Tower at the opposite end. The great gatehouse was joined to the top of the shell keep on the old motte by a stone wall. A recessed path on the top of the wall made it possible to pass from gatehouse to motte in secret and in safety.

The Battle of Bannockburn in 1314 had a direct impact on Tonbridge and on its castle, since in that encounter Gilbert, the last of the de Clare family, was killed. With his death the direct line of descent from the original Richard de Tonbridge, a line which stretched back two and a half centuries, was finally ended. The new lord of Tonbridge was Hugh de Audley, to whom the king, Edward II, granted the right to levy tolls on the crossing of the ford for three years, the proceeds to be spent on enclosing and paving the town. Doubtless Hugh also took an interest in the work being done on the parish church, where the northern arcade of the nave and the north aisle were being built, as was the lower part of the west tower.

By this time the priory was reaching the zenith of its influence and importance, its prior having been given visiting authority to oversee other Augustinian houses. He also received a summons to attend a general council of the order in 1318. In 1333 a mandate was issued to the priors of Tonbridge and Canterbury to visit all the Augustinian houses in the dioceses of Canterbury and Rochester and to deal with all matters relating to their conduct. As was the case with most medieval religious communities, there were frequent squabbles with other religious bodies and with the secular authorities, most of them relating to money or to the ownership of, or authority over, property.

Sadly, the great days of the priory were soon ended. On 11 July 1337 (though, again, various authorities have reservations as to the exact date) the whole priory, including the church and vestry, the library, refectory, dormitory and other buildings, was burnt to the ground, and the vestments, furniture, documents and books, together with the stocks of corn and hay, were all destroyed. A petition asking for urgent help for the brethren also noted that, in addition to the extensive damage and loss caused by the disastrous fire, the priory was situated near a river which frequently flooded their lands, making access impossible. Richard, the original founder, had obviously not been wise, nor perhaps generous, in his grant of the land on which the priory was built. Grants, indulgences and appropriations were all used to rebuild the priory and the following years appear to have been relatively uneventful and financially comfortable, at least.

By the end of the first quarter of the 14th century the population of the area was increasing, people were shaking off some of the old restrictions of earlier medieval times, and the trader was becoming an important person in local society. At about this time, too, there is a suggestion that a bridge spanned the river, at least over the main stream. Iron working developed in the area and a 1325 inventory mentioned six bellows in need of repair, six tuyeres (nozzles, usually of earthenware, through which air was blown into a forge fire), three hammers, two chisels, an anvil, an iron fire, and a branding iron used to mark the king's cattle, all at the Castle Forge. In the same year 7,000 nails and clenches for ship building were made in Tonbridge and sent to Portchester.

By the second half of the 14th century and into the 15th Tonbridge was in the middle rank of Kent towns, its importance stemming from its position as a growing communications centre for the trackway and its ford, and from the river which was starting to be used by boats taking Wealden products to be sold at Maidstone and beyond. It now had a well established market and the people were engaged in agriculture, commerce, iron working and the manufacture of cloth from local wool.

The 16th century was a time of very great change, in many ways a watershed between the old medieval days and the start of modern times. The execution of the Duke of Buckingham for high treason in 1520 broke the centuries-old tradition of warrior nobles holding Tonbridge and its castle, a tradition never to be resumed. The great age of faith had also gone. Everywhere, the religious communities were decreasing in size, and Tonbridge priory was reduced to seven or eight occupants.

Cardinal Wolsey developed a plan to found a new college in Oxford. In order to raise the necessary funds he obtained papal permission to suppress a number of religious houses, of which Tonbridge was one, and to transfer their rights and holdings to the new college. The people of Tonbridge protested, not wishing to lose their priory, even though Wolsey offered them a school in return, from which suitable scholars should have exhibitions to his new college. The protests were to no avail. On 8 February 1524 William, the last prior, was summoned to Westminster to surrender his office as prior of Tonbridge to Wolsey's agent, William Burbank, who then dissolved the priory and granted its assets to Cardinal's College, Oxford, in the following year. The inmates were transferred to other religious houses.

Soon after, on the fall of Wolsey, the priory and its assets reverted to the king, who granted it to the dean and chapter of Windsor in 1532. The monastic buildings fell into decay, so the town lost its priory and did not get the promised school. The loss of the priory which, like most such religious institutions, offered temporary sustenance and refuge for travellers, coupled with the increasing importance of the town as a trading and communications centre, made alternative provision for travellers essential, and the famous old *Chequers Inn* is said to date from this time.

The survey and valuation of the Duke of Buckingham's estates, following his execution in 1520, reports on his Tonbridge holdings as follows:

> In the Lordship of Tonbridge in Kent, is a castle which hath been, and yet is a strong fortress, for the three parts thereof; and the fourth part on the south side being fortified with a deep running water, was intended to have been made for lodgings, and so resteth on 26 feet height, builded with ashlar, and no more done thereunto. The other three parts of the castle being continued with a great gatehouse or first entry, a dungeon and two towers are substantially builded, with the walls and embatelling with good stone, having substantial roofs of timber, and lately well covered with lead, except one half of the dungeon was uncovered.
>
> And as unto the said gatehouse, it is as strong a fortress as few be in England, standing on the north side, having a conveyance, and well embatelled on both sides, to the said dungeon on the west side; and on the south-east side there is a like conveyance to a fair square tower, called Stafford Tower, and from thence to another fair tower standing upon the water nigh to the Town Bridge, being builded eight square and called the Water Tower.
>
> This castle was the strongest fortress and most like unto a castle of any other that the Duke had in England or in Wales. The town of Tunbrigge is a burgh, large and well inhabited with people, having plenty of water running through in sundry places ...

It is interesting to know that the bridge was definitely in existence then, and that it was styled 'The Town Bridge'.

The value of the king's manor is also given:

The Borough of Tonbrigge £13 13s. 0d.	
Less expenses and fees £10 12s. 0d.	£3 0s. 11d.
Chamberlain £0 14s. 0d.	
Less expenses £0 7s. 0d.	£0 7s. 0d.
Bailiff of the meadows and pastures £7 9s. 0d.	
Less expenses £2 0s. 0d.	£5 9s. 0d.
Mill of Tonbridge £10 0s. 0d.	
Less expenses £4 11s. 0d.	£5 9s. 0d.
The total amount being	£14 5s. 11d.

Wyatt's rebellion in 1554, a protest against the marriage of Queen Mary to the Roman Catholic King of Spain, attracted many men from Kent, including some from Tonbridge. In the following year the dreadful Marian religious burnings commenced and claimed two local victims, Joan Beach of Tonbridge, burnt at Rochester, and widow Margery Polley of Pembury, burnt at Tonbridge.

Many remarkable men have figured in the town's long story, but few more remarkable than Sir Andrew Judd, who was born in Tonbridge and became an apprentice of the Skinners Company in London, progressing to become its master six times. He crowned his public life by becoming Lord Mayor of London, a most signal honour. Like so many successful men of his time he remembered his birthplace and, in 1553, he obtained a charter to set up 'The Free Grammar School of Sir Andrew Judde, in the Town of Tunbridge'. He vested control in the Skinners Company, and endowed it with land he bought in St Pancras, and Gracechurch Street, London. There was room for some 50 or 60 pupils who, to obtain places in the school, had to be able 'to write competently and read Latin and English perfectly'. It was granted a number of benefactions over the years but remained small, attracting mainly local patronage until the 19th century.

In the second half of the 16th century many people were dependent upon agriculture and horticulture. Other sources of employment were shipping Wealden produce down river to Maidstone and beyond, providing for travellers, the extraction of local sandstone, and the manufacturing of bricks and tiles from local clay. Weaving continued, some of the cloth being made for the London market, as is indicated by records of fines inflicted there for quite minor defects in cloth offered for sale, a very usual problem for weavers. In 1565 and 1566 a Tonbridge weaver was fined for such offences. Iron working was also an important local industry and records show that in the 1570s Sir Thomas Fane owned one furnace, and Davy Willarde had two forges and one furnace in Tonbridge.

There are various suggestions of bridges, and one record of 1525 mentions a bridge of freestone, 104 feet long, which was then recently built. Could this perhaps have been the Town Bridge referred to in the survey and valuation of the Duke of Buckingham's estates in 1520?

This was a time of great poverty and Sir Thomas Smythe, dealing with gratuities in his will, recorded:

> I do also give to the Parish of Tonbridge toward the maintance of the poor for the year ensuing, Ten Pounds and 8s., with the direction that the Minister and Church Wardens of that parish, or some of them provide weekly twelve fourpenny loaves of good bread, and give it every Sabaoth day at the Church to twelve of the poorest and honestest, in their opinion, dwellers in the Parish, which doe frequent the Church to hear Divine Service and Sermons, and doe receive the Blessed Sacrament of the Lord's Supper, as the Laws of the Land doe appoint. And because the Parish of Tonbridge is of Large Extent and hath many poor inhabitants in it, I desire that my gift of bread in it may be distributed to four and twenty poor people, Viz, to twelve of the poorest on the 1st. Sabaoth, and to other twelve the next Sabaoth, and the first twelve the third day, and so interchangeably to continue from Sabaoth to Sabaoth ...

In the first half of the 17th century the castle passed to Sir Peter Vanlore, a city merchant. His son was a supporter of Charles I in the Civil War, but the sympathies of the people of the town were with Parliament. They were once more involved in conflict not of their own making when in 1643 a Royalist force of about 3,000 men assembled at Sevenoaks and was approached by a Parliamentary force under Colonel Brown. The Royalists retreated and took cover in Tonbridge where they received a demand for their surrender, but they replied that 'they stood for their ancient laws and customs, without which they refused to lay down their arms, but were willing to treat'. Colonel Brown replied that he would come himself to treat with them and ordered his men to attack. After some skirmishing and a little hard fighting, Tonbridge was once more in Parliament's hands, the Royalists losing some dead and 150 prisoners, among whom was a very senior Royalist, Sir George Sandys. A little later a force of some 500 Royalists assembled at Yalding, a few miles away, but Tonbridge people, almost all of whom were Parliamentary supporters, dispersed them. From that time onwards the town was held for Parliament under one of its leading citizens, Thomas Weller, a local lawyer. He received orders from Parliament to 'slight' the castle, and he dismantled it sufficiently to prevent it being of any future military value.

Though Swedenborg, writing in the 18th century, reported that a large furnace near Tonbridge was casting two cannon a day, each weighing 15 cwt., by 1740 only four furnaces were still working in the whole of the county, and by the end of the century cloth making was almost finished throughout the Weald. A development of considerable importance was the authority given to the Medway Navigation Company to modify the river from Tonbridge to Maidstone, to improve its capacity to float commercial barges up and down river. Consequently, in the 1740s it was deepened where necessary and its banks were built up, locks were installed at intervals and landing stages built. Barges of up to 40 tons could now ply up and down the river and Tonbridge became the terminus from where Wealden produce could be shipped down to Maidstone, the barges bringing back goods for the town's shops and market, and large quantities of coal from the coal wharf at Maidstone, where the seagoing colliers discharged their bulk coal cargoes. Thus the loss of the old iron working and woollen industries began to be made good by the expansion of new commercial undertakings and by the increase in trade outside the town.

Religious dissent, beginning in the middle of the 16th century, was now very strong in the town. The priest of the parish church, Edward Ashburnham, was sequestrated for continuing to support the king and the Church of England. The great majority of the townsfolk supported Parliament and were strongly Presbyterian, though there were also a number who belonged to other dissenting bodies. After the restoration of Charles II in 1660, however, the Presbyterians, Anabaptists and the Quakers were much persecuted, but survived and their numbers and influence grew.

Travel was increasing and the popularisation of the chalybeate springs to the south of the town added to its attractions. The *Rose and Crown* was certainly operating as a posting inn at this time, and probably even earlier. Travel became easier when the first turnpike in Kent, running through Tonbridge from Sevenoaks to Pembury and Tunbridge Wells, was opened in 1709-10. Despite the increase in trade, there were still many desperately poor people in the town, for whom the large workhouse was built in Bank Street under the Parliamentary Act of 1723, which authorised the construction of workhouses in parishes. The exact date of the Tonbridge house is recorded as 1733.

The middle of the 18th century saw not only a rise in population, but also a renewed interest in church affairs. In his will George Hooper, a local scrivener, left £500 to 'new and pave' the parish church. The old three-decker pulpit and the horsebox pews, discarded by Ewan Christian during his extensive modifications to the church in the years 1877-79, were then fitted. In 1774 eight bells, cast at the Whitechapel bell foundry, were hung in the tower and in 1788 the first organ was installed. In 1751 a group of Independents worshipped in the town and 40 years later they built their own church, which still survives as the Corn Exchange in Bank Street.

After the middle of the century the coaching trade received a further boost by the introduction in 1784 of a government mail coach service which used the town as a staging post, where horses could be changed and passengers provided with food and refreshments, as they had been for many years by the independent coach operators. Tonbridge's new bridge, replacing an earlier one in 1775, was built to deal with the increase in road traffic through the town. Hasted, the great Kent historian, writing in the latter years of the 18th century, was rather uncomplimentary about this bridge, and also noted that at that time there was a fine vineyard in the castle grounds, and that at Old Forge Farm, which was an iron foundry in Queen Elizabeth's time, there was a mill used 'for the manufacturing of that sort of gunpowder, usually called battle gunpowder ... in 1763 an act passed to enable the proprietors to continue to work the mill as a pestle mill, which is otherwise prohibited by law'.

From the later years of the century onwards the country was again troubled by threat of war, this time the invasion of the south of England by Napoleon's legions, and in Tonbridge a troop was raised as part of the Kent Yeomanry.

In 1800 Tonbridge was still basically a small market town governed by the parish vestry, a stage for the horse-drawn traffic on the London to Hastings turnpike, and in essence little more than an overgrown village without any modern conveniences, health care, sewage disposal or decent housing for many of its citizens who, in consequence, suffered repeated epidemics of diseases now almost eliminated. By the beginning of the First World War it developed into a modern town with all the major amenities and immeasurably better living conditions for its growing number of citizens.

A major breakthrough came with the building of the South-Eastern railway line from London which reached Tonbridge in 1842 and continued through Ashford and Folkestone to Dover, linking the town with the capital and with the south-east coastal towns and the channel ports. A branch line from Tonbridge reached Tunbridge Wells in 1845 and Hastings seven years later, and in 1868 a more direct line to London was built through Sevenoaks. These new railway lines revolutionised both passenger travel and goods transport, and at Tonbridge the junction of the lines brought a considerable increase in commercial activity and a consequent lessening of the earlier insularity of its people.

The main horse-drawn coaches and wagons suffered severely and road travel declined, though locally the old forms of transport continued to be used to connect the country districts with the new railway passenger and goods terminals. The water-borne traffic on the river, though it survived until after the end of the 19th century, went into a decline from which it never really recovered.

A number of the older commercial activities, among them the manufacture of Tunbridge ware, the building and repair of horse-drawn vehicles, the breeding, shoeing and stabling of large numbers of horses, and the servicing of travellers at the Tonbridge Stage, declined and many gradually died out, though the manufacture of bricks and tiles, leather, gunpowder and cricket balls all survived, as did brewing, corn milling, building and printing.

The population increased and considerable numbers of new houses were constructed at both the northern and southern ends of the town, bringing increasing demands for all kinds of building materials and for the craftsmen to use them, needs which were largely met locally. Fine houses, many of which still survive, were built for middle class and business families, most of them to the north of the river. The area south of the river, between the waterway and the railway, became increasingly crowded with poor, small houses huddled together far too closely, accommodating the rapidly increasing numbers of working people. There the conditions became very unsatisfactory, with no adequate sewage disposal or water supplies except from frequently polluted wells close by.

In consequence, there was much illness and indeed major epidemics occurred. There were serious outbreaks of smallpox in 1832, 1838, 1853 and 1878, and of cholera in 1832, 1834, 1838 and 1854. Outbreaks of less virulent diseases such as diphtheria and the more common, if less lethal, diseases were also very frequent.

The town's many problems were insoluble because the ancient system of local government in Tonbridge, as in other places, was vested in the parish, a system which worked reasonably well in small medieval communities but was totally inadequate for the running of an emerging 19th-century town. At last, after much opposition from supporters of parish pump politics, and the setting up of committees to deal with specific problems, the Tonbridge Local Board was set up in 1870 and this organisation did an enormous amount of good work before it, in its turn, was superseded by the Tonbridge Urban District Council in 1894.

Sanitation was much improved in the 1870s when a proper system of sewage was put in hand and an isolation hospital for people suffering from infectious diseases was provided. At this time, too, the old market, granted in 1318, which had come to attract numbers of undesirables into the town, was finally abolished. This period was also to see the adoption of the principal essential services. The streets were first lit by gas in 1836, gas being supplied by the gasworks built that same year in Medway Wharf Road. Electricity was much later in arriving. The generating station was built at the Stade and started to provide electricity for the town in November 1902. The first telegraph connection with the outside world was by the railway system in 1844 and 30 years later the Post Office telegram service was providing services for the general public. The telephone service developed slowly from very small beginnings in the last decade of the 19th century but did not really make an important breakthrough until well on in the 20th. The water supply company was in existence from 1852 when the waterworks opened, but made slow progress in its early years with only 176 customers, increasing to nearly 4,000 by the end of the century.

The Local Board introduced a scheme for the improvement and widening of the High Street to the south of the river where it was very narrow, with no building line and with a hotch-potch of shops and houses on both sides, most of them mean, dirty, decaying and in many cases mere slums. The Board obtained a Parliamentary order in 1893 for the demolition of old properties which were replaced by new shops and better houses. The narrow 1775 bridge was also demolished and replaced by the fine new Big Bridge in 1888.

Tonbridge School first came into being under a charter of 1553 granted to Sir Andrew Judde for the setting up of a grammar school for boys of Tonbridge, his family home. In a brief historical Introduction such as this it would be impossible to attempt a detailed account of the school. It remained small, catering principally for local boys until the early years of the 19th century, and it was housed in a simple two-storey rectangular building, though dormer windows in the roof indicate that the roof space was also used. Modest additions to the building were made in the late 18th century but from 1825 progress was almost continuous and under Dr. James Welldon, headmaster between 1843 and 1875, the number of pupils increased more than fivefold. It was during his time, in 1863-64, that major alterations took place. A new range of buildings, set well back from the public road, was completed and the old school was demolished.

Welldon was succeeded by the Rev. Theophilus Barton Rowe, during whose headmastership much additional building work was carried out. The school became a public school in 1888, attracting pupils from far afield. During subsequent years additional buildings, including the central tower, Big School and science laboratories were added. The lovely school chapel, now alas a burnt ruin, brought a fitting conclusion to the principal building operations before the commencement of the First World War. Progress continues and it is now one of the outstanding public schools in the country.

The creation of the public school attracted pupils from a wide area and this of course reduced the number of local boys who could be admitted, although the school had originally been founded for their benefit. After much argument and the consideration of many schemes for the education of local boys, the Judd Commercial School was set up as a temporary expedient in Stafford House in East Street. It proved very successful, and the Judd School, still standing in Brook Street, was opened in 1896 and much extended later. It is now partnered, on the opposite side of the street, by the West Kent College.

This period was also notable for the amount of church building and reconditioning carried out. The parish church of SS Peter and Paul was reconditioned in 1820 (the main south aisle probably dates from this time) and again in 1878-9 when the outer south aisle was added and the whole building was subjected to a brutal 'restoration' during which so much of the old furniture and fittings, the heritage of many centuries which we would treasure today, was wilfully destroyed. St Stephen's church was built and enlarged, together with St Saviour and several missionary rooms and temporary buildings.

The Wesleyan Methodists, present in the town from the beginning of the century, erected modest buildings in Swan Lane, now renamed East Street, in 1829. In 1872 they erected their present church on the same site which, having survived almost unchanged, is a fine example of its type. The United Methodists built their church in Priory Street in 1868 to replace an earlier one in the same street. Other places of worship built in this period were the Strict Baptist chapel in Pembury Road, the Baptist and Congregational churches in the High Street, and several other mission halls and temporary buildings in various parts of the town. Salvation Army members built their citadel in Lyons Crescent in 1898 and the Roman Catholics erected their temporary church in Waterloo Road, before building a permanent one in Lyons Crescent in the early years of the 20th century.

To supply the many licensed houses in the town there were two principal breweries, the Bridge Brewery on the south side of the river close to the Big Bridge, and the Royal Victoria Brewery.

A most important event for the town was its purchase of the old castle and its grounds in 1897-8, the council taking it over in 1900. The grounds formed a fine open space next to the Big Bridge and the High Street, and the mansion adjoining the old gatehouse provided accommodation for the various council departments and offices.

The 19th century ended on a sombre note with the outbreak of the Boer War, some of Tonbridge's young men being involved. The tablet on the war memorial in the Castle Walk lists the names of 24 men who died in that campaign, some of them local citizens, the others old boys of Tonbridge School. There were to be two more wars in the 20th century. The First World War involved the service, suffering and death of many Tonbridge men, and the Second World War also took its toll of the youngest and fittest of the local men. The sky over the town was a battleground where many of the encounters between the R.A.F. and the Luftwaffe were fought out. The quiet Garden of Remembrance, with its comprehensive memorial, is a tribute to them all.

The period between the two World Wars was a time of great difficulty and depression. It was also, however, a time when the groundwork for much future progress was laid. Printing developed considerably, as did various forms of light industry, the manufacture of building materials and house building itself. The terrible fire at the Whitefriars Press did enormous damage, as did recurrent river floods which afflicted the low-lying part of the town between the Big Bridge and the railway. The 1930s saw the end of production at the gunpowder mill just outside the town.

One very important event was the purchase by the town of the old racecourse, so called because horse races had been held there from time to time. As a consequence of this far-seeing purchase, Tonbridge obtained 50 acres of land adjoining the south-west of the castle grounds which the council already owned. On this land a noteworthy recreation ground was created, cricket, football and bowls grounds were laid out, and children's playgrounds, a swimming pool, a miniature railway track and other amenities were provided. This recreation ground is the envy of many larger and richer communities who possess nothing to rival it.

There are too many post-war developments to deal with in a brief survey of this kind. However, some mention must be made of the building of new factories for the increasingly important light industrial firms, and the building of the new bypass, without which the High Street would long since have been quite impassable. The gas and electricity enterprises became merged in national monopolies, electricity ceasing to be produced at the Stade in 1951. Gas production has also ceased in the town.

Church developments included major alterations to the parish church, where the largely unused outer south aisle and the area at the rear of the nave were converted into upper and lower floors, the empty space so created being arranged to provide meeting halls, quiet rooms, office space, a kitchen and a canteen area, necessary facilities to fit the church for its modern ministry in the community. The old Congregational church in the High Street was pulled down and replaced by the modern Christ Church on the same site, and the old High Street Baptist church was also demolished, a new building on the corner of Darenth Avenue and Derwent Road being built to replace it.

In spite of the failure of many schemes in the past to control disastrous flooding, records of which survive from as early as the 14th century, it was resolved that something more must be done, so in July 1968 the Kent River Authority commissioned a feasibility study of possible methods to eliminate flooding completely. Two months later, in September 1968, the worst flood in living memory took place, and no longer was theoretical research needed. All the material was suddenly there, needing only to be recorded. The acceptance of a detailed report on the necessary measures in 1974 led to the River Medway (Flood Relief) Act of 1976 which gave the signal for work to commence.

A giant flood storage reservoir, using the Medway valley down river from south of Penshurst near where the Medway and Eden rivers join, was created by building an earthen flood barrier, some 300 metres long and in places as much as 5.7 metres high, across the Medway valley above Tonbridge. This reservoir will hold surplus water above it, from which it can be released at a rate sufficient to prevent flooding lower down river through a control structure in the barrier. This control structure contains a modern sluice with three radial gates which releases water into a new channel, dug just to the north of the railway line. The old river bed, passing south under the railway and then following a winding course before joining the main river at the end of the Long Reach, is thus bypassed. The scheme was commissioned in 1981 and the total cost of the project was £3.6 million.

The area adjacent to these developments has been made into the Haysden Country Park, which includes two artificial lakes – Haysden Lake on which the Tonbridge Town Sailing Club is based, and Barden Lake which started life as a gravel pit. The old winding river bed, now bypassed by the main river, is called The Shallows and forms a fine nature reserve. The country park contains quiet footpaths, a picnic area and a car park.

Two important administrative developments must be mentioned before the conclusion of this brief, and necessarily incomplete, survey. The first was the creation, under the Local Government Act of 1972, of the Tonbridge and Malling District by uniting the Tonbridge Urban District with the Malling Rural District and the parishes of Hadlow and Hildenborough. This enlarged authority was to be developed further nine years later when, in December 1983, the Lord Lieutenant of Kent presented the Royal Charter granting the district the status of a borough. Councillor Barry Hughes, chairman of the district at the time, had the enviable and unique distinction of being both the last chairman of the old district and the first mayor of the new borough.

Such are the bare bones of Tonbridge's long story. Very early local residents lived short, harsh, brutish lives in rough shelters beside the river or in the Iron Age forts on the hills to the south. Centuries later, following the Battle of Hastings, they were rounded up to provide forced labour to build the Norman upstart's earthen castle. Now the people own the castle and live comfortable lives, free people in a free modern town, part of a borough by virtue of a royal charter granted by the queen, and presided over by a mayor, a member of the borough authority they freely elected by secret ballot.

Old Maps

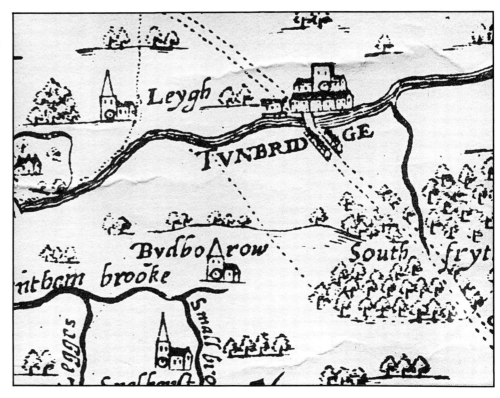

1. This section of Symonson's map of 1596 shows the castle gatehouse, the parish church and the bridge.

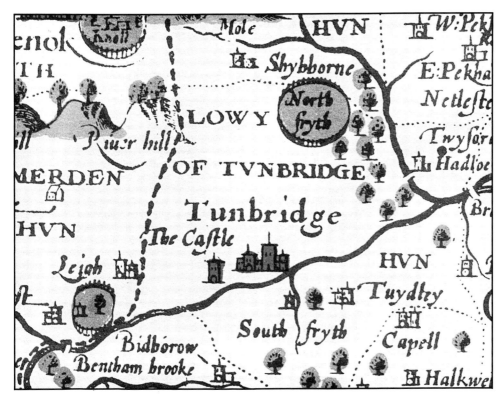

2. Part of a 17th-century map which illustrates the 'Lowy of Tunbridge', the North Frith and the South Frith.

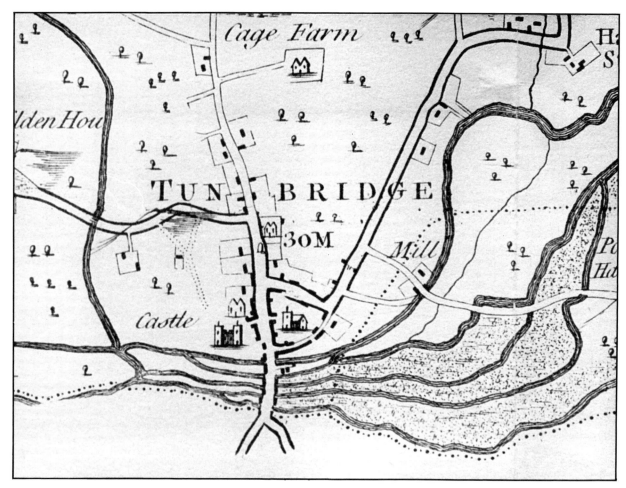

3.   Part of the late 18th-century map which was used by Hasted in his *History and topographical survey of the County of Kent*. The five streams which flowed through the town are clearly shown, as are the castle gatehouse, the church and the mill.

The Castle and Gatehouse

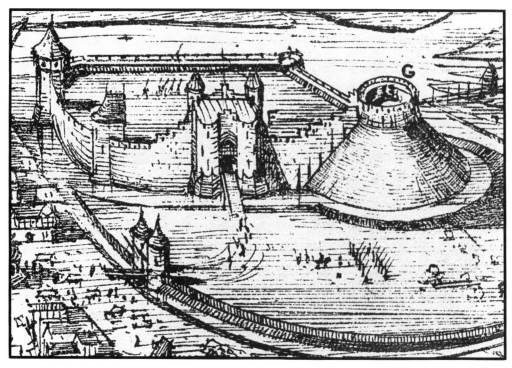

4.   This drawing by J. F. Wadmore, A.R.I.B.A., shows what the castle may have looked like *c*.1260. The 11th-century motte, surmounted by its shell keep and surrounded by a moat, is clearly shown on the right. James Foster Wadmore, who died in 1903 aged 81 years, was an architect, a local historian and a fine draughtsman. He lived in Tonbridge, designed many local buildings and published fine drawings of the town.

5.   Another drawing by James Foster Wadmore, showing the castle as it must have appeared in medieval times. On the right is the motte with its shell keep, connected to the gatehouse by means of a curtain wall which contained a shielded passageway between the two. The central entrance through the gatehouse was reached over a moveable wooden bridge.

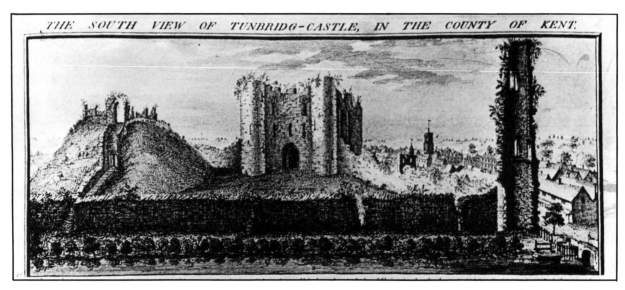

6. This 1735 drawing entitled 'The south view of Tunbridg- Castle in the County of Kent' is by Samuel and Nathaniel Buck, who produced many fine illustrations of Kent. On the left is the motte surmounted by the ruins of the shell keep, in the centre is the gatehouse and just to the right the parish church. At the bottom is the river and at the extreme bottom right the bridge.

7. The castle gatehouse *c.*1787. The house which now stands beside it had not then been built, the old moat had been filled in at the front of the gatehouse, and stone is being carried away for use elsewhere in the town.

8. The castle gatehouse as shown in *Our Own Country* vol. 1,
published *c*.1880.

9. The interior of the ruined gatehouse as it was in the
19th century, when drawn by James Foster Wadmore.

10. A 1989 view of the castle from the Big Bridge when the southern section of the perimeter wall was undergoing maintenance work.

11. Looking down from the curtain wall of the shell keep on top of the motte. From here in medieval times the lord or one of his personal bodyguards would have kept watch on his somewhat unreliable hired mercenary soldiers billeted in the bailey below. The shell keep, some of which survives, was built mainly of sandstone blocks, a material then in good supply locally.

12. The west side of the gatehouse, showing the remains of the curtain wall which connected the gatehouse doorway to the top of the motte. The sides of this curtain wall were extended upwards, protecting anyone using the path along the wall from enemy fire.

13. The north or outer side of the gatehouse. The moat, which originally passed in front of it, was at this point crossed by a moveable bridge. This section of the moat was filled up in the 18th century.

14. (*above*) The well inside the shell keep, vital to the inhabitants of the castle.

15. (*right*) The passageway through the gatehouse, both ends of which were fitted with a stout door and portcullis.

16. (*below*) An old muzzle-loading gun outside the north of the gatehouse. Its surface is very badly pocked, suggesting that it has suffered a long period of exposure to the elements.

17. A view of the south side of the castle gateway and the house adjoining it. The building of the house was begun by Thomas Hooker and completed by William Woodgate of Summerhill, who then gave it to his son as a wedding gift. The estate was purchased in 1897-8 by the local authority, which took possession of the whole property in 1900.

18. The council chamber given over to an exhibition of the Tonbridge Art Group in July 1989 – a splendid setting for such an event.

Public Services

19.   The gasworks. The streets of Tonbridge were first lit by gas on 12 November 1836. The local
gas company was later taken over by the South Suburban Gas Company, and is now part of the
South Eastern Gas Company.

20.   A water company was in existence from the early 1850s when the waterworks was opened, but then only 176 houses
were connected to the mains, other houses relying on water from wells, many of which were polluted. There were several
campaigns to persuade the local authority to purchase the water company but 'parish pump politics' prevented this and
today it forms part of the West Kent Water Company.

21.   Part of the sewage treatment system in Vale Road.

22.   The early fire service was the responsibility of the old Lighting and Watching Committee which used the base of the tower of the parish church in which to store their two manual fire pumps, thatch hooks for pulling blazing thatch off buildings, and other simple fire-fighting equipment. The old thatch hooks still remain in the church tower. Later, part of a building in the High Street, also used as a library and council offices, served the same purpose, the old manual pumps being housed in a separate building.

23. In 1901 this purpose-built fire station was built in Bank Street and a proper town fire brigade was formed, consisting of one professional fire-fighter and 20 volunteers. A salamander steam pump was bought and stored at the station, drawn by horses to fight local fires. The later fire-fighting lorry was much more mundane, if more efficient. Later still a petrol-driven fire engine replaced the earlier pumps.

24. The old fire station still survives in Bank Street, as does this memorial stone built into its front wall. Dealing with fires is now the responsibility of the Kent Fire Brigade which has a station in Vale Road.

25.   The Tonbridge Urban District Council Fire Brigade in 1937.

26.   This photograph of the Tonbridge division of the Kent County Constabulary probably dates from the second half of the 19th century. Some of its members were of generous proportions and were obviously able to enforce the full weight of the law!

27.   The Tonbridge division of the Kent County Constabulary in March 1899. The officer standing at the extreme right, wearing a bandolier and a sword, is the division's mounted member.

28.   The Tonbridge division of the police force in 1912.

The "Lady Davenport" Challenge Trophy for Life-Saving.

WINNERS, 1937 - TONBRIDGE DIVISION.

B. C. FLEMONS   TONBRIDGE.

P.C. CANNON,   P.C. EDMONDSON,   P.C. LINCOLN,   P.C. SUTHERLAND,
P.C. BOYER,   Insp. F. C. McKAY,   Supt. S. W. POLLINGTON,   P.C. MacPHERSON,   P.C. GILES,
                                                                        (Instructor),   (Captain),

29.   The Tonbridge division team, winners of the Lady Davenport life saving challenge trophy in 1937.

30. This building at the Slade was erected to house the electrical generating equipment which started to produce current in 1902. The machinery consisted of two vertical steam-engines driving generators producing direct current at 220-240 volts, and supplemented by a storage battery. Additional plant was required from time to time as demand steadily increased, and this included another steam-engine and generator, two diesel and one steam turbine plants with their associated equipment. Coal for the steam boilers was brought up the river and unloaded near the works.

31. The generation of electricity at the Slade works ceased in 1951. When the generating equipment was removed this part of the engine room was partitioned off to become the Milne Museum, housing a large collection of electrical appliances of all kinds, from generating and distributing equipment to commercial and household appliances. Sadly, it will soon close and become part of a museum in Sussex.

Houses of Refreshment

32.   For many years the *Angel Hotel*, on the corner of the High Street and Vale Road, was·a distinctive feature to everyone approaching the town from the south. It was demolished when the area was redeveloped in the 1970s and the Angel Leisure Centre was built.

33.   The *Ivy House*, on the corner of Bordyke and the High Street, was earlier known as the *Elephant and Castle* and is one of the oldest Tonbridge inns.

34. The *Man of Kent*, a timber-framed inn in East Street. Part of the front is clad with Kentish weatherboard and the end is tile hung.

35. The Courtyard Restaurant, a timber-framed building adjoining the *Man of Kent*, has a tiled roof with fine old dormer windows. It is situated in East Street, originally known as Swan Lane, one of the very old roads in the town.

36. The *Rose and Crown* is a timber-framed coaching inn with an 18th-century façade which hides the wooden framing. Its porch stretches out across the pavement and was traditionally the place from which election results were announced. The arms are of the Duke and Duchess of Kent, parents of Queen Victoria. The *Rose and Crown* was an important stopping point for the horse-drawn coaches and carriages which travelled from London through Tonbridge and on to the coast in the 18th and early 19th centuries.

37. This rear view of the carriage entrance of the *Rose and Crown* shows part of the old timber-framed construction of the original house.

38. A drawing of the *Chequers* c.1904, by Hugh Thomson. Thomson illustrated Walter Jerrold's *Highways and Byways in Kent*, published in 1907. The *Chequers* was probably built in the late 15th century and is a fine example of a Kentish timber-framed house with front-facing gables.

39. The *Chequers* in pre-motoring times.

40. The *Chequers Inn*, looking up the High Street from the Big Bridge. Like the *Rose and Crown* opposite, it was a posting house for the horse-drawn carriages in previous centuries and, again like the *Rose and Crown*, it still welcomes travellers today.

Tonbridge Buildings

41. This early 18th-century building which stood in the High Street is sadly now gone. Thomas Day, who carried on the Stidolph business, demolished it in 1878 and erected in its place a more imposing building. When producing such drawings, especially of business premises, artists frequently drew people, horses and carriages disproportionately small, to make the premises appear much larger and more impressive than they were.

42. The Old Ivy House in East Street, originally two separate homes before it was converted into a single dwelling called the Portreeve's House. It is a fine timber-framed house of the late 15th or early 16th century and, according to tradition, was once the *Old Swan Inn* which gave its name to Swan Lane, now East Street. It is also said that it was once the home of the gatekeeper of the gate which gave access to the town from the meadows to the east.

43. The Portreeve's House in East Street, earlier known as the Old Ivy House and now beautifully preserved as one of the finest old houses in the town.

44. An early timber-framed house in Church Lane.

45. Church House at the end of Church Lane, near the entrance to the church. Built in the 18th century, it has a Kentish weatherboard ground floor, a tile hung first storey, and a tiled roof incorporating dormer windows.

46.   The much drawn and photographed house, long since a shop, next to the *Chequers* and built on a narrower frontage. The two forward-facing gable ends abut each other, and curved corner braces give a pleasing and symmetrical appearance to the building. The ground-floor shop front is a more recent alteration to what is undeniably a beautifully planned façade.

47.   A High Street survivor. This part of an old weatherboarded house, now turned into a shop, forms a pleasant contrast to the modern shops all round it.

48. One of the fine buildings to survive in the High Street, to the north of the Big Bridge. Above the ground-floor doors and windows the words 'London and County Bank' can still be faintly seen. The first reference to this bank in the town appears in 1836.

49. This building, on the corner of Pembury Road and St Stephen's Road, is now the Kent Music Centre.

50. The Pembury Road Almshouses, dated 1874.

51. This fine building in Bank Street was built in 1723 as the town's workhouse. It served this purpose for many years until a new workhouse was built at Pembury. In 1845 it was opened as a school which survived until the 1960s when the remaining pupils were transferred elsewhere. For several years it remained empty and was badly vandalised, but it has now been restored and converted into offices.

52. Ferox Hall, a 16th-century house to which a Georgian front was added at the beginning of the 19th century. It was much altered in 1878 and is now the property of Tonbridge School. It has had many distinguished occupants, including several generations of the Children family. It was during the occupation of this old Kentish family that Sir Humphrey Davy, the famous scientist, often stayed at the house.

53. The Priory in Bordyke. This house was never actually a priory and in the 18th century it was called 'Chauntlers'. It was home to several famous local people, among them Thomas Weller, a lawyer who was a leading citizen during the Commonwealth, and a supporter of Parliament. Another owner was Eliza Acton (1799-1859). Her cookery book, published in 1845, and her bread book which followed in 1857, were pioneering efforts in the field of cookery-book publishing.

54. The Hermitage, a 16th-century building, another of the town's treasures.

55.   The library, built in 1900 as a 'Free Public Library and Technical Institute'.

56.   Built in 1874, the Public Hall has served many purposes. At various times it has been used for public meetings, as a cinema and as a bingo hall.

57.   The Oast Theatre. The building, a working oast-house until 1966, was opened as a theatre on 20 April 1974 by Lady Rupert Nevill. The conversion was done by Bell & Company (Westminster) Limited, and by the owners, the Tonbridge Theatre and Arts Club.

'Wise's Tunbridge Ware'

58. From the 18th century onwards the Wise family lived in Tonbridge and ran 'Wise's Tunbridge Ware Manufactory', producing small- and medium-sized wooden farings and ware and, later, articles of furniture, many of them decorated with attractive contemporary views. These pieces are now much sought after and fetch high prices. Wise's Manufactory was at the north-east corner of the Big Bridge and is illustrated in the two right hand roundels, the upper one showing its front elevation facing the High Street, and the lower one the side of the building facing the river. They published illustrations of contemporary views which were used to decorate their productions. The four roundels shown here, and the four following illustrations, are examples of their set of Tonbridge views.

59. Wise's view from the Big Bridge, looking up river.

60. Wise's view of the old castle gatehouse.

61. View up the High Street to the north, from the Big Bridge. The building on the right is the Wise Manufactory.

62. Wise's view of the High Street, looking to the north. The town hall on the left was built early in the 19th century. The *Chequers* lies behind it to the extreme left.

Street Scenes

63.   A late 18th-century or very early 19th-century view of the town from the Tunbridge Wells road.

64. An old drawing of the junction of Bank Street with the High Street.

65. An old photograph of the junction of Bank Street with the High Street. Perhaps it was one of Mr. Cooke's photographs.

66. Church Lane, one of the town's ancient thoroughfares, with the medieval tower of the old parish church of St Peter and St Paul at the far end.

67. The view northwards up the High Street, before the demolition of the old town hall in 1901. Even though the road was widened as a result, it is a pity the building was lost.

68. A close-up view of the narrow road between the *Chequers* and the old town hall. Note the gas street lamps.

69. The old market place was that part of the High Street outside the *Chequers*, shown on the left of this picture. In the centre of the market place stood this quaint old building, open at ground level and with a loft in the roof space entered by a door in the gable end. Nearby stood the stocks and whipping post – justice was very public in those days! This drawing is unsigned but is identical with one used in Arthur Neve's book on Tonbridge, signed G.E.M., George Mackley the distinguished Tonbridge wood engraver and water colourist (*see* Plate 72).

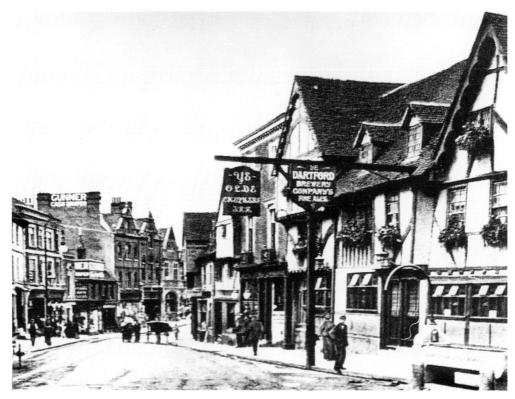

70. An old view, looking southwards down the **High Street** towards the **Big Bridge**. The cattle drinking trough is shown in its former position at the bottom right.

71. The High Street in 1989. Queensway has replaced the *Angel Hotel* and a plethora of modern cars now crowds the street where once only the occasional horse-drawn vehicle was seen.

The Railway

72. The original railway station which served the town from 1842 until the present station was built in 1868. This drawing was by George Mackley. A similar picture appeared in Arthur Neve's book on Tonbridge, published in 1934 and now long out of print. Mackley was born in Tonbridge in 1900 and educated at the Judd School before going on to train as a teacher at Goldsmith's College, London. He taught in a number of schools before becoming headmaster of Thames Ditton Primary, and then of Sutton School, from which he retired at the end of his teaching career. He both taught and practised art, becoming well known for his wood engraving, which was the title of his classic book on the art, first published in 1948 and re-issued twice in the 1980s. He illustrated other books, including *Weeds and Wild Flowers*, published in 1965, and Neve's book on Tonbridge. His work was shown at many Royal Academy exhibitions and he was elected to many artistic bodies. In 1961 he was elected a Fellow of the Royal Society of Painter-Etchers and Engravers. He was created an M.B.E. in January 1983, only a few weeks before he died in February of that same year, aged 82.

73. The front façade of the present railway station. The original station was on the opposite side of the street.

74. The rear of the station building, looking eastwards from the end of Gladstone Road.

The Market

75.   The Corn Exchange in Bank Street, at the entrance to the market, has had a varied life. This was the Independent chapel which was built by the nonconformist group referred to as the 'Congregation of Protestant Dissenters' who, after meeting for some 40 years in a backyard room behind the *White Hart Inn*, erected this building as their church in 1791 and subsequently enlarged and improved it several times. It was sold to the Market Company in 1875, and from 1876 onwards the congregation worshipped in the new Congregational church built at the end of the High Street, near the old *Angel Inn*.

76.   The cattle market in full swing in earlier days. Tonbridge no longer has its own cattle market.

77.   This cattle drinking trough, a boon to the many animals once driven on foot to the market, now stands in the High Street, just south of the *Chequers*.

78. The modern Tonbridge markets, held on Saturdays, are for food, clothes and other consumer goods, but not livestock. They are a riot of colour and attract large crowds.

79. The market butcher always has a constant flow of sales patter, attracting an audience both of customers and fascinated onlookers.

Churches and Chapels

80.   An interesting 19th-century view of the parish church from the north-west. Smoke billowed out from many chimneys in those days.

81. The north side of the parish church of St Peter and St Paul, showing the earliest of the three nave aisles, the 14th-century north aisle. The south aisle was added during the 1878-9 renovations and enlargement.

82. The parish church from the north-east. The round-headed windows in the chancel wall at the left of the picture are part of the surviving early work, probably of the 11th or early 12th century. Note the great east window, whose glass was destroyed by enemy action in the Second World War.

83. A photograph of the parish church before the many alterations in the late 1870s. Note the old galleries, the three-decker pulpit and the horsebox pews, all lost during those renovations.

84. A similar view, looking to the west. Note the organ in its old position in the west gallery.

85. A 19th-century drawing of the interior of the parish church, looking to the west before the 1877-9 alterations.

86. A recent view of the interior of the nave of the parish church, looking to the west. The modern partition which shuts off the nave from the base of the tower is seen at the far end.

87. A drawing of St Stephen's church in Victorian times. The great increase in population in the southern part of the town, following the opening of the railway in 1842, led to the building of St Stephen's 10 years later.

88. An early photograph of St Stephen's. Note the scarcity of traffic and the ever-present horse and carts, which carried modest loads at very slow speeds.

89. A recent view of St Stephen's. Its tall, slender spire is a local landmark.

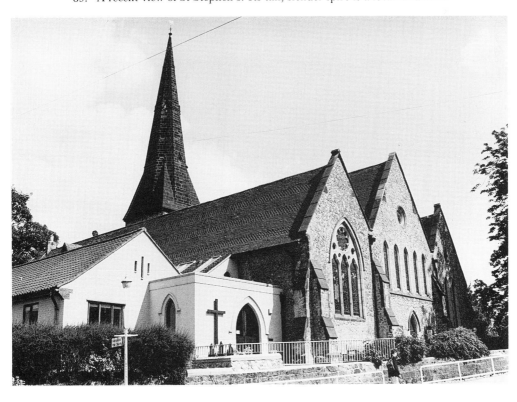

90. The interior of St Stephen's church, a most successful example of Victorian Gothic.

91. In the decade before the First World War stained glass windows were presented to St Stephen's church in memory of the Chippindale family. This example is considered to be very successful early 20th-century work.

92. The St Stephen's group of the Campaigners, a uniformed Christian organisation, in the 1950s.

93. St Saviour's church in Dry Hill Park Road was built in 1875 for worshippers who preferred the High Church and Anglo-Catholic form of service. It is a simple brick building with a semi-circular apse at its eastern end.

94.   The Wesleyan Methodists worshipped in the town early in the 19th century and built a small chapel and school accommodation in Swan Lane, later renamed East Street. In 1872 the present church, shown here, was erected and its fine interior survives almost in its original state.

95.   The memorial stone in the wall of the Methodist church in East Street. Messrs. C. Punnett and Sons constructed many buildings in the town and district.

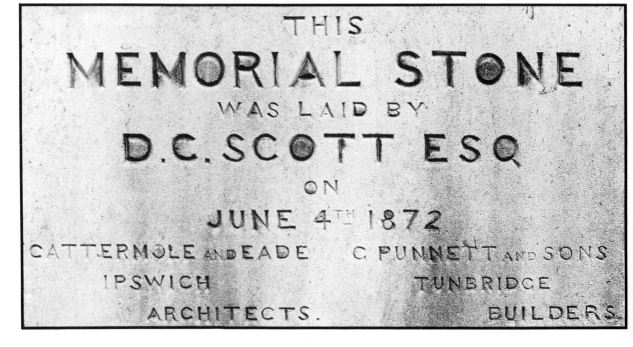

THIS
MEMORIAL STONE
WAS LAID BY
D.C. SCOTT ESQ
ON
JUNE 4TH 1872
CATTERMOLE AND EADE   C. PUNNETT AND SONS
IPSWICH   TUNBRIDGE
ARCHITECTS.   BUILDERS

96. Corpus Christi, the Roman Catholic church in Lyons Crescent, was built in 1904 to replace a temporary building in Waterloo Road.

97. The interior of Corpus Christi church.

98.   The old Congregational church which stood in the High Street, and to the right, the *Angel Inn*. Both buildings have now been demolished. The church, built in 1875-6, was pulled down in 1978 and replaced by the modern Christ Church.

99.   This pulpit, which originally stood in the old Victorian Congregational church, was saved when that building was demolished, and installed in the new Christ Church.

100. The old Baptist church in the High Street was opened in 1872 and its front remodelled in 1903. It suffered severely in the disastrous flooding of 1968 and was later sold and demolished, the congregation moving to a new modern building in Darenth Avenue.

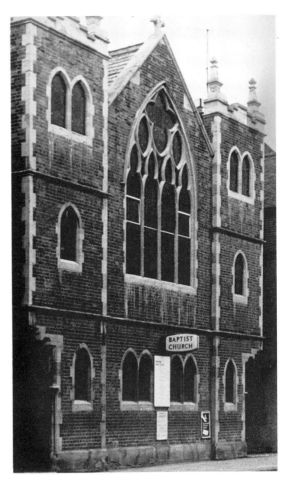

101. The interior of the new Baptist church, a brick building which includes a hall and offices.

102. The Strict Baptist chapel in Pembury Road was built by the prolific Tonbridge builder, George Punnett, in 1867.

The Priory

103.   One of J. F. Wadmore's drawings of the surviving Priory buildings, *c*.1830. This may have been the remains of the Priory chapel.

104.   The old Priory ruins as they were *c.*1800.

105.   Another of Wadmore's drawings of the remains of the Priory buildings around 1830. Note the building at the rear which had been converted into a brass and iron foundry.

The Judd Bequest

106. An early, but undated, view of the original grammar school buildings.

107. A drawing of 'Tunbridge School' by T. Richards.

108. 'The Grammar School, Tunbridge, Kent. Drawn by T. M. Baynes. Engraved by H. Adlard. Published July 1830 by Geo. Virtue, 26 Ivy Lane.' These three men, Baynes the artist, Adlard the engraver, and Virtue the printer and publisher, produced many fine drawings of Kent in the 1830s.

109. 'A view of the Grammar School at Tonbridge in Kent. From a picture painted and presented to the Worshipful Company of Skinners, London [governors of the school] by Jonah Smith Wells Junr. Esqr. Master 1831.'

110. An early Victorian view of the front of the school, identical in its details with the line drawings published in 1830.

111. 'The Cricket Match, Tonbridge School', published in 1851. The school has always had a strong cricketing tradition.

112.   The rear of the school buildings as they were between 1827 and 1863.

113. A fine old print of the upper school as it appeared until 1864.

114.   The interior of the school chapel before the disastrous fire.

115.   The Tonbridge school chapel in 1989. This fine building, erected in the first decade of the 20th century, was reduced to a ruined shell by fire.

116. A rear view of part of the school buildings, showing the central tower.

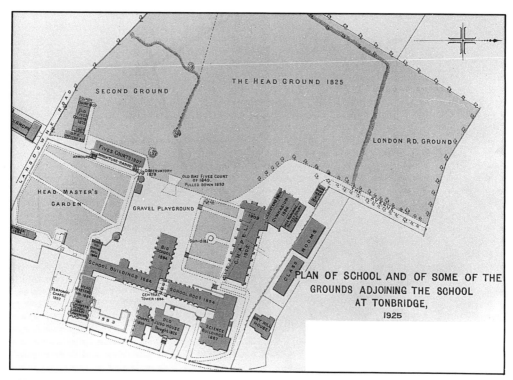

117. A 1925 plan of the school and grounds, now preserved in the school library. It records the dates when the principal buildings were erected.

118. The school library, photographed in 1989.

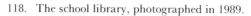

119. Stafford House in East Street, the first home of the Judd School, founded there in 1888.

120. The Judd School in Brook Street in 1989. The school was opened in 1896, extended in 1930-1, and subjected to further improvements later. It was the permanent successor to the temporary Sir Andrew Judd Commercial School which opened in East Street in 1888.

121. The original staff of the Judd School. Seated, from left to right, are: T. E. Grice, W. J. D. Bryant (Headmaster) and
E. W. Handcock. Standing, from left to right, are: C. J. Kimmins, G. Nunn, C. E. E. Shill and H. A. Grindrod.

Sir Andrew Judd's
Commercial School

(Close to Tonbridge Railway Station).

❖

INSTRUCTION given in all the Subjects needed to fit Boys for Commercial Life.

FEES: for Boys entering under Ten, **£2** per Term up to the age of Twelve. For all other Boys, **£2 10s.** per Term.

These Fees are inclusive of all charges for Books, Stationery, Games, Library, and Carpentry Tools.

Dining Accommodation is provided for Boys coming from a distance.

SEASON TICKET RATES Charged by S.E. Railway

for Boys under 15 years of age attending the Tonbridge Schools.

Second Class for Three Months—dating from any Day.

FROM THE FOLLOWING STATIONS TO TONBRIDGE.	RATE.			GOVERNMENT DUTY	
	£	s.	d.	s.	d.
Hildenborough	0	15	0	0	9
Sevenoaks	1	5	0	1	3
Dunton Green	1	10	0	1	6
Brasted	1	14	0	1	9
Westerham	1	16	0	1	10
Penshurst	0	18	0	0	11
Edenbridge	1	8	0	1	5
Godstone	1	16	0	1	10
Paddock Wood	1	0	0	1	0
Yalding	1	7	6	1	5
Wateringbury	1	10	0	1	6
East Farleigh	1	10	0	1	6
Maidstone	1	16	0	1	10
Horsmonden	1	10	0	1	6
Goudhurst	1	13	0	1	8
Cranbrook	1	16	0	1	10
Marden	1	12	6	1	8
Staplehurst	2	0	0	2	0
Tunbridge Wells	0	17	6	0	11
Southborough	0	12	6	0	8

Scholars over 15 and under 18 pay one-third more.

N.B.—As each School Term comprises as nearly as possible 13 weeks, three payments, made at the beginning of the several Terms, will cover the charge for the whole School year.

122. This early leaflet provides an interesting comparison with present day travel costs. Note that the prices listed here are for three months.

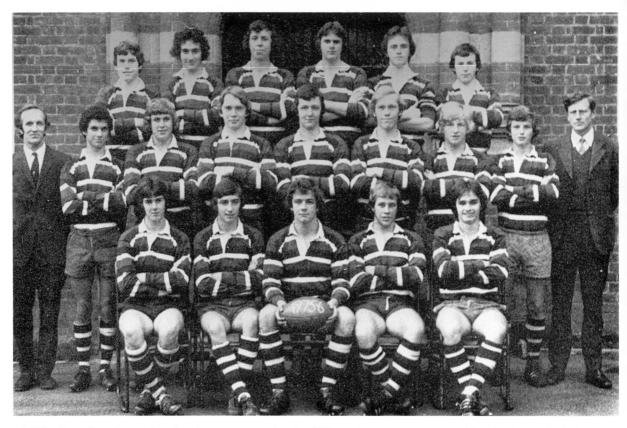

123. Sport has always played an important part in school life, and team games are considered to be particularly important. This is the Judd School rugger XV, which achieved the distinction of remaining unbeaten during the 1975-6 season.

124. The West Kent College in Brook Street, a modern building which serves as an area centre for further education. It is situated opposite the Judd School, in the same road.

Memorials

125.   The memorial to the dead of the Boer War in the gardens beside the Castle Walk, between the river and the bailey wall of the castle.

Erected
by friends to the
memory of those whose
names are inscribed below.
Townsmen of Tonbridge
or
Old Boys of Tonbridge School.
They loyally gave their lives for Queen
and Country, and fighting in the War
against the Boers, helped to save
South Africa for the Empire.
1899 – 1902.
"Their bodies are buried in peace,
but
Their name liveth for evermore"

Col. G.E. Lloyd.   Col. C.F. Lindsell.
Col. W.F. Curteis.   Capt. M. Kortright.
Lieut. W.J.C. Fletcher.   Lieut. R.C. Wiltshire.
Arthur T. Beeching   Frederick S. Black
William Black   Richard Brigden
F.H. Brittain   Henry H. Carter
Geo. E. Edmonds.   Geo. Humphrey
A.E.H. Logan.   William Lucas.
H.W. Masterman.   Jos. R. Maday.
Frederick Read.   E.N.E. Smart.
A.J.R.G. Smart.   J.A. Tolhurst.
Herb. Twort.   F.W. Cox.

126.   The panel in this memorial contains 24 names of men of Tonbridge and old boys of Tonbridge School who lost their lives in the Boer War.

127. This memorial commemorates the dead of two world wars, and is situated at the end of the Garden of Remembrance, a quiet corner in part of the public grounds near the river walk.

THESE GATES
WERE ERECTED
IN MEMORY OF
THE
OLD BOYS
OF
THE JUDD SCHOOL
WHO GAVE
THEIR LIVES
IN THE WAR
OF
1939-45

128. The panel affixed to the gates of the Judd School in Brook Street.

129. This panel can be seen high up on a wall on the west side of the High Street, just to the south of the Big Bridge. Frank Woolley was one of the legendary cricketers of Kent and England fame. A great left-handed batsman and a fine bowler, he played 764 matches and 64 tests and his record is awesome. He scored a total of 58,969 runs and took 2,068 wickets in first class matches, and became a revered father-figure to young sportsmen.

130. On the interior wall of the outer south aisle of the parish church of St Peter and St Paul is this memorial tablet to another Kent cricketer, Colin Blythe. He volunteered for the army during the First World War and after much service was killed at Ypres in November 1917. 'As cricketer, soldier, patriot, he played the game.'

Whitefriars Press

131.   For many years Tonbridge has been an important centre for printing. This Whitefriars Press building on the south bank of the river, just below Big Bridge, was photographed in 1989, when the firm's transition to other sites in the district was under way, but not yet completed.

132.   This old print of Whitefriars was captioned: 'View of the original building [centre with sloping roof]. Office Block extension on the extreme left, three-floor extension on the right and ground floor Machine Room etc. in the foreground. Taken from the back of the Works looking North-West. The bushes and trees in the foreground show the course of the back-stream before it was diverted.'

133.   The three founders of the Standard Catalogue Company Limited and the Whitefriars Press Limited. Left, Mr. S. S. Dottridge; centre, Mr. E. Noel Barker (Chairman); right, Mr. C. Percy Moss. This appears to be the only surviving photograph of the three founders.

134. The Whitefriars bindery and warehouse staff in 1925. The workers are all dressed in overalls or aprons except the four people in the centre of the front row, the two men being overseers and the two ladies supervisors.

135.   The Whitefriars Jobbing Composing Department. This photograph shows part of the original printing works established by Bradbury, Agnew & Company Limited in 1896.

Flooding

136. Tonbridge has been subject to flooding for centuries. This rather faded postcard shows Danvers Road in the 1911 floods.

137. The last great flood occurred in 1968, and this photograph, taken by Mr. G. E. Hall, is entitled 'Off to work! at the back of Tonbridge Railway Station'.

138. Mr. Hall's photograph of the 1968 floods outside the *Angel Hotel* in the High Street, nearly opposite the library. The *Angel* has since been demolished.

139. Flood water in the High Street, looking from the railway station to the Big Bridge.

The River and its Bridges

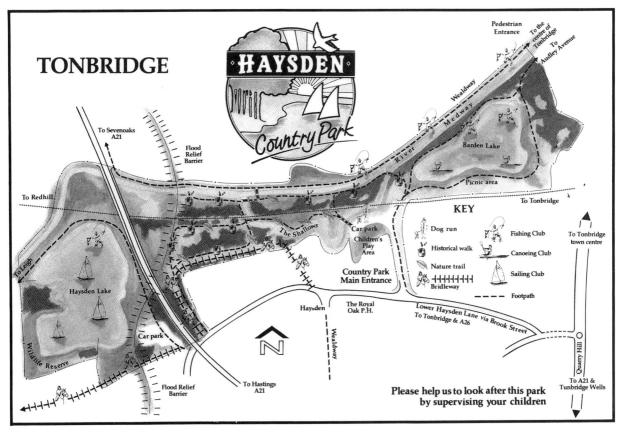

TONBRIDGE

HAYSDEN
Country Park

Pedestrian
Entrance
To the centre of Tonbridge
To Audley Avenue

To Sevenoaks
A21

Flood
Relief
Barrier

Wealdway

River Medway

Barden Lake

To Redhill

Picnic area

To Tonbridge

To Leigh

The Shallows

Car park
Children's
Play
Area

KEY

Dog run

Historical walk

Nature trail

Bridleway

Fishing Club

Canoeing Club

Sailing Club

Footpath

To Tonbridge
town centre

Haysden Lake

Wildlife Reserve

Car park

N

**Country Park
Main Entrance**

Haysden

Wealdway

The Royal
Oak P.H.

Lower Haysden Lane via Brook Street
To Tonbridge & A26

Quarry Hill

Flood Relief
Barrier

To Hastings
A21

**Please help us to look after this park
by supervising your children**

To A21 &
Tunbridge Wells

140.   The Borough's attractive information board at the Haysden Country Park shows the various attractions provided here. The winding stream labelled as 'The Shallows' was the original bed of the river until the straight 'New Cut' was excavated to bypass it. The position of the flood relief barrier is also shown.

141.   The new Tonbridge bypass road crossing the Medway valley. In the distance is the Tonbridge town sailing club on Haysden Lake, one of the two artificial lakes in the Haysden Country Park.

142.   A train passing over the six-arch railway bridge on its way to London. This bridge is on the northern bank of Haysden Lake.

143. This twin-arched bridge carries the railway over water which, before the new cut was made, was part of the winding course of the old river bed.

144. Lucifer Bridge is an iron footbridge over the main river from Barden Park at the end of Audley Avenue. After crossing the bridge, a left turn will take the walker westwards along the river bank, passing the Haysden Country Park on the opposite side of the river, and thence to the control structure of the flood barrier.

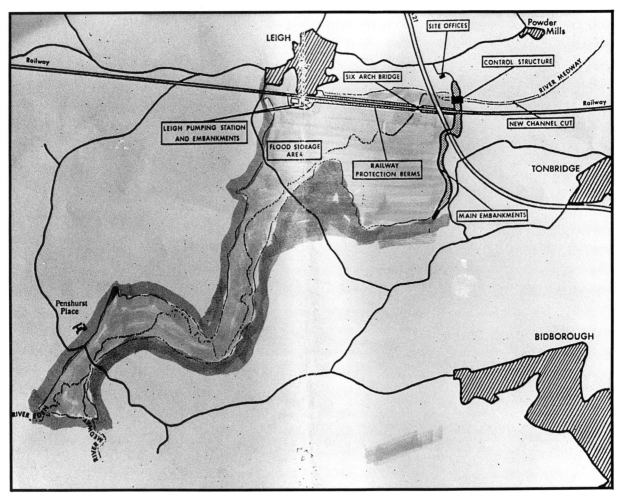

145. The shaded area of this map, reproduced here by courtesy of the Tonbridge offices of the National Rivers Authority, shows the flood storage area in the valley of the river Medway.

146. A view from up river of the control structure. It is a massive reinforced concrete sluice, containing three radial sluice gates operated by sophisticated control gear, and designed so that its overall height was kept to the minimum to avoid environmental damage to the valley.

147. The control structure, looking up river, with the central radial sluice gate partly open.

148. Craft of the Tonbridge town sailing club add interest to Haysden Lake, one of the two artificial stretches of water created in the Haysden Country Park. The second was Barden Lake.

149. Looking across the river to the gardens and gatehouse of the castle. In the foreground is a Tonbridge Waterways craft, which operates the Caxton river cruises, a splendid way to see the town.

150.   Looking up river from the Big Bridge.

151. An interesting old drawing, unsigned and simply captioned 'The brewery and bridge, Tonbridge'.

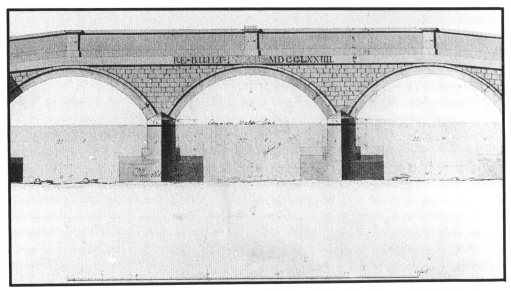

152.   The elevation of a design for 'the new intended bridge at Tunbridge', drawn in 1774 by Robert Milne (1774-1811). The bridge was built in 1775 and demolished when the new Big Bridge was erected in 1888.

153.   This engraving by Walton was made from an original drawing by P. Saxby. It shows the 1775 bridge with the castle in the background. Hasted, the late 18th-century historian, recorded that: 'There was built in 1775, on the foundations of the former one, which was grown ruinous, a new stone bridge of three arches, which cost eleven hundred pounds, at the County's expence. It was built from a design of Mr. Milne, but is calculated more for utility than ornament.

154.   The Big Bridge in 1989, looking down river from the north bank of the river Medway. An early record states that the town bridge was erected in stone in 1526, and that the town's bridges were repaired at county expense in 1628. There have been several bridges across the river at this point, variously styled as town bridge, principal bridge, great bridge, and big bridge. The usual name today is Big Bridge.

155.   The Big Bridge looking up river from the north bank. Note the elaborate supporting brackets beneath the roadway. A cast-iron plaque records the iron founders as Gray Bros., 1887. The bridge was widened at that time and re-opened in September 1888 by the council chairman, Mr. M. D. Cornfoot.

156. Looking up river to the town lock, just down river from the Big Bridge.

157. A cabin cruiser passes up river through the town lock.

158. Lyons Wharf, on the north bank of the river, near the Big Bridge. Though it has been converted into a restaurant, much of the original character and appearance of the building has been preserved.

159. The Little Bridge, looking up river.

160. Looking up river at Cannon Bridge, just yards from the gasworks and modern industrial buildings.

Festivals and Ceremonies

161. The 1989 May Festival: the Chamber of Commerce entry crosses the Big Bridge.

162. A very appropriate entry in the carnival day procession was that of the Tonbridge Young Farmers, since the town has long prospered as a market town providing services for local farmers.

163. One of the carnival day events staged on the lawn in the shadow of the 13th-century gatehouse, which makes the perfect backdrop for a play with historic associations.

164. A clog dancing group performing on the castle lawn, not during the May Festival, but at the celebrations following the formal part of the Freedom in the same month.

165.   The mayor, Councillor G. Horne, inspects the Queen's Regiment during the Exercising of the Freedom of the Borough of Tonbridge and Malling. The inspection was held in the High Street on 13 May 1989.

166. The mayor and Major C. Argent prepare to inspect the band.

167. Representatives of Tonbridge and Malling Borough Council and of 5 Queen's (V) on Tonbridge castle lawn during the Exercising of the Freedom of the Borough. From left to right are: Major and Mrs. C. L. Argent, Mr. and Mrs. J. E. Sweetman, Mayor Councillor G. Horne and Mrs. Horne, Brigadier H. N. Tarver, and Lieutenant-Colonel and Mrs. P. L. Pearce.

168. The opening ceremony of the Tonbridge town sailing club at Haysden Lake in the 1970s by the chairman of the district council.

169. Prince Edward opening the extension to the Tonbridge Oast Theatre on 22 April 1988. The photograph is by Brian Barnes.

170.   The mayor of 1989-90, Councillor Mrs. Billie Sinclair-Lee, accompanied by Major John Sinclair-Lee, at one of her first mayoral engagements at the parish church of St Peter and St Paul.

Borough Status

171. The document recording the Privy Council's recommendation to the Queen that a charter be granted to Tonbridge and Malling. As a result the Queen ordered '... a Warrant to be prepared for Her Majesty's Royal Signature for passing under the Great Seal a Charter in conformity with the said Draft which is hereunto annexed'.

At the Court at Buckingham Palace

THE 19th DAY OF OCTOBER 1983

PRESENT,

THE QUEEN'S MOST EXCELLENT MAJESTY
IN COUNCIL

WHEREAS there was this day read at the Board a Report of a Committee of the Lords of Her Majesty's Most Honourable Privy Council dated the 13th day of October 1983 in the words following, viz:—

"YOUR MAJESTY having been pleased, by Your General Order of Reference of the 20th day of June 1973, to refer unto this Committee the humble Petition of the council of the district of Tonbridge and Malling, praying for the grant of a Charter under section 245 of the Local Government Act 1972.

"THE LORDS OF THE COMMITTEE, in obedience to Your Majesty's said Order of Reference, have taken the said Petition into consideration and do this day agree humbly to report, as their opinion, to Your Majesty, that a Charter may be granted by Your Majesty in terms of the Draft hereunto annexed."

HER MAJESTY, having taken into consideration the said Report and the Draft Charter accompanying it, was pleased, by and with the advice of Her Privy Council, to approve thereof and to order, as it is hereby ordered, that the Right Honourable Leon Brittan, one of Her Majesty's Principal Secretaries of State, do cause a Warrant to be prepared for Her Majesty's Royal Signature for passing under the Great Seal a Charter in conformity with the said Draft which is hereunto annexed.

N. E. Leigh

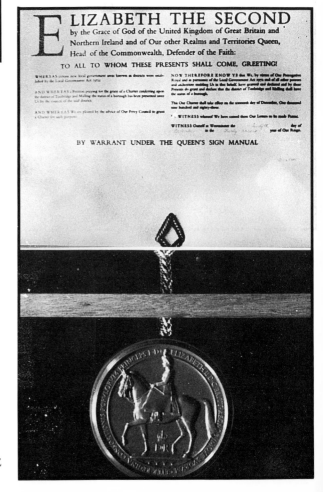

172. The declaration granting borough status under the Queen's signature and seal. 'Now therefore know that we ... have granted and declared and by these presents do grant and declare that the district of Tonbridge and Malling shall have the status of a borough. BY WARRANT UNDER THE QUEEN'S SIGN MANUAL.'

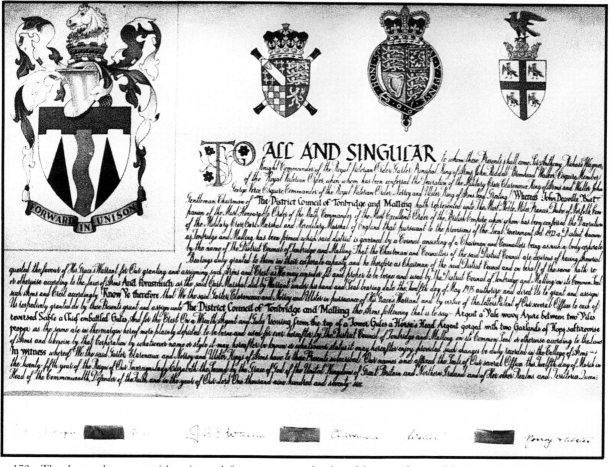

FORWARD IN UNISON

TO ALL AND SINGULAR to whom these Presents shall come, Sir Anthony Richard Wagner Knight Commander of the Royal Victorian Order, Garter Principal King of Arms, John Riddell Bromhead Walker Esquire Member of the Royal Victorian Order upon whom has been conferred the Decoration of the Military Cross, Clarenceux King of Arms and Walter John George Peter Esquire Commander of the Royal Victorian Order, Norroy and Ulster King of Arms send Greeting Whereas John Deaville Brett Gentleman Chairman of The District Council of Tonbridge and Malling hath represented unto the Most Noble Miles Francis Duke of Norfolk Premier of the Most Honourable Order of the Bath Commander of the Most Excellent Order of the British Empire upon whom has been conferred the Decoration of the Military Cross Earl Marshal and Hereditary Marshal of England that pursuant to the provisions of the Local Government Act 1972 a District known as Tonbridge and Malling has been formed which said district is governed by a Council consisting of a Chairman and Councillors being as such a body corporate by the name of The District Council of Tonbridge and Malling That the Chairman and Councillors of the said District Council are desirous of having armorial Bearings duly granted to them in their corporate capacity and he therefore as Chairman of the said District Council and on behalf of the same hath requested the favour of His Grace's Warrant for Our granting and assigning such Arms and Crest as may be proper to be borne and used by The District Council of Tonbridge and Malling on its Common Seal or otherwise according to the Laws of Arms And forasmuch as the said Earl Marshal did by Warrant under his hand and Seal bearing date the twelfth day of May 1975 authorise and direct Us to grant and assign such Arms and Crest accordingly Know Ye therefore That We the said Garter, Clarenceux and Norroy and Ulster in pursuance of His Grace's Warrant and by virtue of the Letters Patent of Our several Offices to each of Us respectively granted do by these Presents grant and assign unto The District Council of Tonbridge and Malling the Arms following that is to say - Argent a Yale wavy Azure between two Piles reversed Sable a Chief embattled Gules And for the Crest On a Wreath Argent and Sable issuing from the top of a Tower Gules a Horse's Head Argent gorged with two Garlands of Hops both reversed proper as the same are in the margin hereof more plainly depicted to be borne and used for ever hereafter by The District Council of Tonbridge and Malling on its Common Seal or otherwise according to the Laws of Arms and likewise by that Corporation by whatsoever name or style it may hereafter be known or whatsoever status it may hereafter enjoy provided such changes be duly recorded in the College of Arms - In witness whereof We the said Garter, Clarenceux and Norroy and Ulster, Kings of Arms have to these Presents subscribed Our names and affixed the Seals of Our several Offices the twelfth day of March in the twenty fifth year of the Reign of Our Sovereign Lady Elizabeth the Second by the Grace of God of the United Kingdom of Great Britain and Northern Ireland and of Her other Realms and Territories Queen Head of the Commonwealth, Defender of the Faith and in the year of Our Lord One thousand nine hundred and seventy six.

173. The charter document with, at its top left corner, a reproduction of the coat of arms of the borough of Tonbridge and Malling.

174. Councillor Barry Hughes after the ceremony of the presentation of the royal charter on 16 December 1983. Councillor Hughes became the first mayor of the new borough of Tonbridge and Malling.

175. Councillor Barry Hughes who had the unique distinction of being both the last chairman of the old district council and the first mayor of the new borough of Tonbridge and Malling.